First Facts™

Community Helpers at Work

A Day in the Life of a
Garbage Collector

by Nate LeBoutillier

Consultant:
Steve Ridzon
Technical Programs Coordinator
Solid Waste Association of North America
Silver Spring, Maryland

Capstone
press

Mankato, Minnesota

First Facts is published by Capstone Press,
151 Good Counsel Drive, P.O. Box 669, Mankato, Minnesota 56002.
www.capstonepub.com

Library of Congress Cataloging-in-Publication Data
LeBoutillier, Nate.
   A day in the life of a garbage collector / by Nate LeBoutillier.
   p. cm.—(First facts. Community helpers at work)
   Includes bibliographical references and index.
   ISBN-13: 978-0-7368-2629-7 (hardcover)   ISBN-10: 0-7368-2629-7 (hardcover)
   ISBN-13: 978-0-7368-4672-1 (softcover pbk.)   ISBN-10: 0-7368-4672-7 (softcover pbk.)
   1. Sanitation workers—Juvenile literature. 2. Refuse and refuse disposal—Juvenile literature
[1. Sanitation workers. 2. Occupations.] I. Title. II. Series.
HD8039.S257L4 2005
628.4'42'023—dc22   2003024651

Summary: This book follows a garbage collector through his day and describes his occupation
   and what his job requires of him.

Editorial Credits
Amanda Doering, editor; Jennifer Bergstrom, series designer; Molly Nei, book designer;
   Eric Kudalis, product planning editor

Photo Credits
All photos by Capstone Press/Gary Sundermeyer except page 20 (left), Atlantic Sales and Salvage
   and page 17, Creatas

Artistic Effects
Capstone Press/Gary Sundermeyer, 4, 6, 15, 19

Capstone Press would like to thank Rick Goff and Waste Management, Mankato, Minnesota,
   for their assistance in creating this book.

Printed in the United States of America in North Mankato, Minnesota.
052011   006176R

Table of Contents

When do garbage collectors start their days?

Garbage collectors wake up early in the morning. They start work when most people are still sleeping. Rick the garbage collector arrives at the office. He picks up his paperwork and swipes his **time card** to start the day.

Fun Fact!

There are about 100,000 garbage trucks in the United States.

4:30 in the morning

5

How important is safety to garbage collectors?

Safety is very important to garbage collectors. Once a week, Rick goes to safety meetings. At the meetings, he learns how to keep himself and others safe on the job.

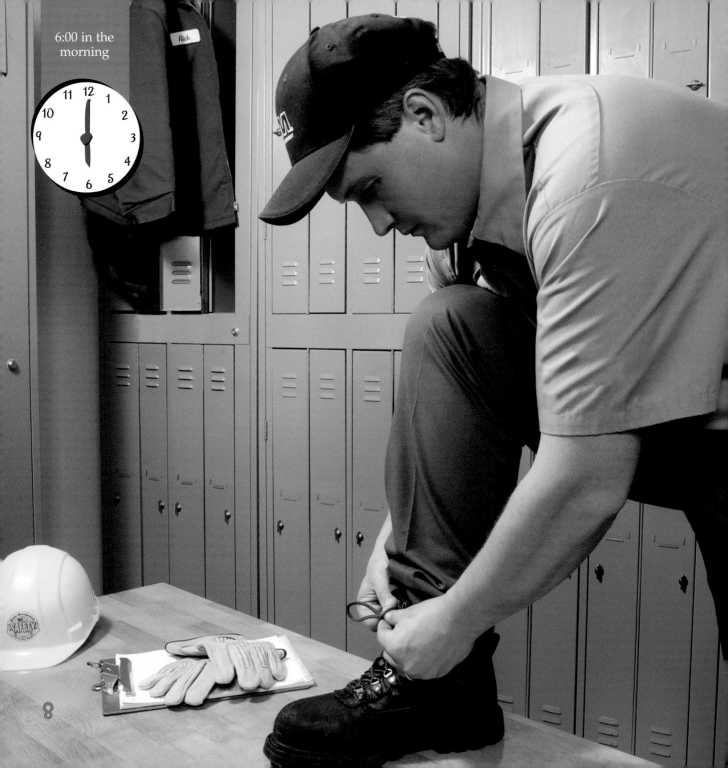

6:00 in the morning

8

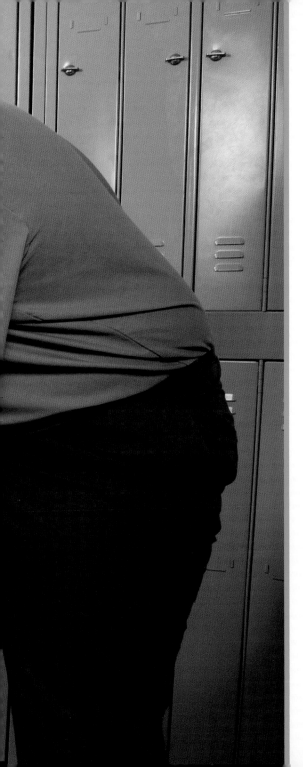

What do garbage collectors wear?

Garbage collectors wear shirts, pants, gloves, and steel-toed boots. Gloves keep Rick's hands safe from sharp objects, such as broken glass. Rick's boots keep his feet safe from falling garbage. Garbage collectors also wear hard hats when they dump garbage.

What do garbage collectors drive?

Garbage collectors drive trucks. The garbage truck has a large bin to hold trash. Rick checks the truck for problems each morning. This morning, he fills the tires with air.

! Fun Fact!
Some garbage trucks have two sets of controls. Garbage collectors can drive from the right or left side of the truck.

WASTE MANAGEME

WASTE MANAGEMENT

(555) 442-1137

What do garbage collectors do?

Garbage collectors drive different **routes** every day. They stop at houses and buildings to pick up garbage.

A lift on Rick's truck picks up
garbage cans. It dumps the garbage into
the truck. The garbage is crushed to
make room for more.

11:30 in the
morning

DUT 308623

14

Who helps garbage collectors?

Mechanics help garbage collectors by taking care of the trucks. Mechanics fix trucks when they break down. Today, Jeremy checks a truck for problems.

People can also help garbage collectors. They can help by putting their garbage neatly into bags and cans.

What happens when the truck is full?

When the truck is full, it is time to dump the garbage. Rick dumps his truck at a holding area.

At some holding areas, the garbage is sorted. Some of the garbage is **recycled**. The rest of the garbage is taken to a **landfill**. At the landfill, the garbage will be covered with a layer of dirt.

2:00 in the
afternoon

How do garbage collectors end their days?

Garbage collectors have work to do after the garbage is dumped. Rick puts fuel in his truck for tomorrow. He fills out paperwork in the office. Rick swipes his time card and goes home to rest for another day.

Amazing but True!

Garbage trucks can be painted any color. Some companies have rainbow-colored trucks. The most popular color for garbage trucks is white.

Shovel

Garbage can

Lift

Hard hat

Safety vest
Garbage collectors must wear brightly colored safety vests in the truck yard and on the route. People can easily see these bright vests.

Gloves

Recycle bin

Glossary

landfill (LAND-fil)—an area where garbage is buried; at a landfill, garbage is stacked and covered with dirt.

mechanic (muh-KAN-ik)—someone who operates or fixes machines

recycle (ree-SYE-kuhl)—to make new items from old items; cans, plastic, paper, and glass can be recycled.

route (ROUT)—a series of places a garbage collector visits to pick up garbage

time card (TIME KARD)—a card used to record the time a worker is on the job

Read More

Brill, Marlene Targ. *Garbage Trucks.* Pull Ahead Books. Minneapolis: Lerner, 2005.

Leeper, Angela. *The Landfill.* Field Trip! Chicago: Heinemann, 2004.

Internet Sites

FactHound offers a safe, fun way to find Internet sites related to this book. All of the sites on FactHound have been researched by our staff.

Here's how:
1. Visit *www.facthound.com*
2. Type in this special code **0736826297** for age-appropriate sites. Or enter a search word related to this book for a more general search.
3. Click on the **Fetch It** button.

FactHound will fetch the best sites for you!

Index